So You Want To Be Prime Minister?

Ben Wicks

So You Want To Be Prime Minister?

McClelland and Stewart

The Canadian Publishers
McClelland and Stewart Limited
25 Hollinger Road, Toronto M4B 3G2

Canadian Cataloguing in Publication Data

Wicks, Ben, 1926–
  So you want to be prime minister?

ISBN 0-7710-8992-9

1. Prime ministers – Canada – Anecdotes,
facetiae, satire, etc. 2. Canada – Politics
and government – Anecdotes, facetiae, satire, etc.
3. Canadian wit and humor (English).* I. Title.

FC173.W53 1984   354.71003′1′0207   C84-099067-7
F1026.4.W52 1984

Printed and bound in Canada

This book is sold on the understanding that
no refund will be given to those who
do not become Prime Minister of Canada.

FOR DOREEN
VINCE
SUE
KIM

So You Want To Be Prime Minister?

You and everyone else.

With a start up salary of over $80,000 a year,
a mansion rent free, food and board
paid by the taxpayer, and a chance to
nip over and take a spot of tea
with the Queen
whenever you feel like it . . .
of course you want to be Prime Minister.

Unfortunately it ain't as easy as all that.
For one thing you'll need friends.
Millions of them. All adults.
They'll need persuading that whatever it is
that you intend to do
will benefit them.

And this is the easy part
of your fight to get to Sussex Drive.

The tough part is knowing the language of politics:
English or French won't help. It's been devised
to keep the likes of you and me from getting
anywhere near the big fat office on the Hill.

The language of politics
is full of boring and vague terms
intended to send newspaper readers
scurrying to the sports section.
Even readers who hate sports.

With this book I intend to unravel
some of the mystery surrounding the nonsense
that is to be found in Ottawa.

So let us begin. And where better than with the letter 'A.'

A

Apathy

It's a disease
carried by the news that an election
is on the way.

Symptoms: Drowsiness and indifference.
Cause: Knowledge that whoever the
voters put into the big chair
will do exactly the
same kind of job
as the one that they have
just tipped out.
Present company excepted,
naturally.

Agenda (a.k.a. Order Paper)

Something that you'll write down and distribute
before the start of a meeting.
The length of it depends on how fast
you need to get away
to more important things,
such as, oh, skiing,
dancing, or more tea
with the Queen.

Autographs

As Prime Minister you'll be asked for yours
wherever you go.
All of them will be for people
who haven't the faintest idea
who you are.
Don't worry about it being legible.
In fact, the less legible, the better.
They might think it is the signature of
Michael Jackson and feel that they have
an autograph really worth keeping.

Here are a few examples that you can follow:

Brooke Shields

The Pope

The Queen

Robert Redford

Michael Jackson

Absent

Most of the members of the House of Commons
when you're not there.
The moment you come out of the woodwork,
so do they.

If you want a bill to get passed in the House, take a trip.
Leave the job to your acting PM.

Where should you go?
Go to London and have more tea
with the Queen.
There are plenty of voting-age Brits
in Canada.
They love this kind of
nonsense.

Americans

People who tell us how much our dollar is worth.
They think Canada is covered with snow
and that our police wear red uniforms
and chase French-Canadian villains
across the Arctic wastes.

The fact that we are just as ignorant about their country is
not the point.

At least we know who their President is.

We've seen him in the movies.

A PRESIDENT

Atomic Energy

It's the energy of the future. And Canada has proven that for only twice the cost it can successfully do the job of oil, of which there is now a surplus.

Acid Rain

It causes fish to die. There are a lot of voters in Canada who would like to kill those fish themselves. Intend to do something about it.

If you're not sure what to do, form a committee.

Attorney General

Pierre Elliott Trudeau was it before he made it
to the top job that you're after.
He made the famous statement that
no one was allowed in the bedrooms of the nation.
Since then no Mountie has entered
the bedroom of any Canadian
without knocking first.

Ambassadors

Most of them will live just around the corner
from your new house on Sussex Drive.
All of them have toadied up to the leader back home
so he would let them live in Canada
in a bloody great mansion rent free.

They give great parties.

What else do they do? No one knows.
But, without them, bad relations would exist
between their country and ours.
They would stop buying our goods
and we would stop buying theirs.

What about the countries
that don't buy anything from us?
These are known as Third World countries.
They also give great parties.
Back in their own countries.

B

Bomb (as in The Bomb)

We don't have one.
We don't need one.
If we do need one,
we can borrow one
from the Americans,
who have promised
to loan us one.

Because we don't
have one,
we are treated
the same as
everyone else who
doesn't have one.
Uganda, Bangladesh,
and Tonga.

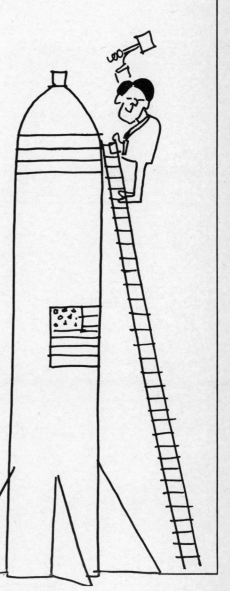

Briefings

They're held wherever you go.
They can be held in a bus,
in a train, or in a plane.
They let you know where you are going,
who you're going to meet,
and what they want you
to do for them.

But don't worry about remembering it.
You can forget all you've been told.
In an hour you'll head
for the next town.

MY FELLOW WHO-EVER-YOU ARE

Ballot

It's your ticket to heaven.

People vote for the person they feel will do:
(a) The best job for themselves;
(b) The best job for the country.

I'M FOR CHERNENKO— THIS IS THE RUSSIAN EMBASSY

So you have a name
that's impossible to spell?
Don't worry about it.
The piece of paper has the names
already written on it.
All the people have to do is put an X
beside the one they fancy.

Ballot Box

It's built like a telephone booth
and has a curtain on one side.
This is the side you go through to get in.
Once inside, the voter
is on his own . . .
or should be.

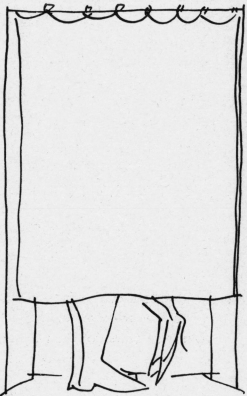

Some people do not enjoy
being alone in a booth.
They become extremely agitated.
This causes panic,
which results in what
are known as spoiled ballots.

People have spoiled ballots by:
(1) Marking of an X beside every name;

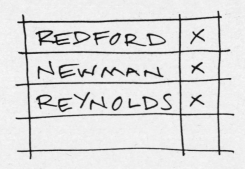

(2) Adding the name of the person who is voting . . .
   and then placing an X beside it;

(3) Adding the name of a person who is not running,
   but who, in the opinion of the voter,
   would do a better job than any of the candidates
   on the ballot: Donald Duck . . .
          Spider-Man . . .
          my wife . . .

   Just because you are
trying to make it to the top job
does not exclude you from voting.
So don't forget to cast your ballot.
It could be the only vote you'll get.

If you get uneasy in confined places, here are a few tips that may help you relax inside the booth:

(1) Take a book.
    Not a thick book.
    There are others waiting.

(2) Take in a musical instrument.
    Not drums.

(3) Now relax. Remember, you are recommending someone for the cushiest job in the world, with so many perks coming under the door that they'll need a shovel to get them into the In tray. When you leave that box your folded piece of paper should look like this.

YES   NO

Backbencher

All members of Parliament promise
to do everything for those who voted for him.
You will find some of them part of your crowd.
Some you like. Some you don't.
Fair enough.
You can't be expected to like everyone.
But does that mean you have
to look at someone you hate
day in and day out for years?
It does not.

You can make him a backbencher.
He's out of sight and hopefully out of mind.

However,
remember that there are times
when you will need him.
Such as
whenever you say something in the House.
At a flick of your finger
he will be required to thump his desk.
(see "How to thump a desk")

He is also expected
to throw his meagre support your way.
There will be times when you will find him
showing signs of getting out of line.
Warn him that any nonsense
will be rewarded with a seat
even farther away from the cameras.

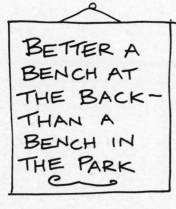

YOU

Regardless of how strongly
he may feel about an issue,
when that bell rings
he'll go into his pavlovian-dog routine
and trot behind you
until the count is done.

BACK
BENCHER

Remind him that a lost vote
can bring about the fall of your
gang and with it his job.

EX
MP

BETTER A
BENCH AT
THE BACK —
THAN A
BENCH IN
THE PARK

Suggested sign for the office of
every backbencher.

How To Thump A Desk

With the palm of the hand. (A)

Doing it with the fingers
can result in broken fingers.
No leader wants a team with
hands that can only make a silly little
tap-tap that wouldn't do justice to Tinkerbell.
The whole idea of thumping a desk
is to make noise . . .
loud noise.

So let's start again from the beginning:
Hold the hand about six inches above the desk
with the palm down.

Now,
with a
nice
sharp
rhythmic
motion,
bring the
palm of the hand down sharply onto the desk top.

Did you hear a nice bang? Good.

Now lift the palm of the hand and repeat the action –
up,
down,
up,
down.
Isn't this fun?

Keep it up . . .
bang, bang, bang . . .

Now start shouting,
"Hear! Hear!"
Louder.
"Hear! Hear!"
Isn't this wonderful?
Hear! Hear! . . .
Bang, bang . . .
LOUDER . . .
BANG BANG . . .
HEAR HEAR . . .
NOW STAND ON
YOUR CHAIR . . .
LOUDER
LOUDER . . .

That's all for today. Now, same time tomorrow. Don't lose your mitts as you run off home to Mummy.

C

IT'S A CONSTITUENT— SHALL I SAY THAT YOU'RE IN A MEETING OR THAT YOU'VE LEFT FOR THE DAY?

Constituent

Someone back home.
Most of them helped you
get where you are.
You owe them something.
So when they write to you
with a problem,
get someone to answer their letter.

If you think that you may know
the person who is writing,
make an extra effort.
Sign the letter.

Constitution

It's something that the Queen had and we shared.
Now we have one of our own.

There are two copies, so in case of fire or theft
there will still be one around to use.

Canadair

The company formed:
(a) to build airplanes, which it did, with taxpayers' money;
(b) to sell aircraft, which it did not.

It may have lost billions of dollars, but it has been able
to help highly paid executives
stay off the unemployment lines.
And away from successful industries.
And voting for you.

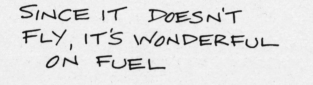

Crown Corporations

Non-profit companies kept alive in order to keep down the
unemployment figures.

Campaign Speech

Your speech written by others, who know exactly what the people you're speaking to want to hear.

Coup

Something that happens in hot climates.
Since this is Canada you have nothing to worry about.

Coup, bloodless

As above, without blood.

Critics

They're everywhere.
Outside your immediate family.

OUTSIDE CRITIC

Inside your immediate family.

INSIDE CRITICS

YES!   NO!

Whatever you do as PM
is going to be wrong.
The trick is to find
the thing that is the least wrong.
This is not easy,
as you have to give the impression
that what you are doing is right,
while knowing full well that
what you are doing is wrong.

Unfortunately,
you have already those who
recognize that you are doing wrong,
that what you are doing is not right.
Try telling everyone that,
although you know
that what you are doing is wrong,
it has every likelihood
of being right.

Most people will feel
that the wrong you promise
will not be nearly as bad
as they imagine.
It may also be better
than what the other camp says is right,
which you say is wrong.

P.M.'s
OFFICE

Children

You love them. Especially your own. Take them with you everywhere. Along with the
nanny,
babysitter,
pediatrician,
and playmate.

They look great in photos with you. The devoted parent willing to sacrifice all his time for the children.

One word of advice:
Just you and the children in the photo.
No nanny,
babysitter,
cook,
maid, or
playmate.

BABY
SITTER
PLAY
MATE
NANNY
PHOTO
WIFE

Cruise Missile

A deadly weapon that can find its way through
valleys and mountains on its own.
For this reason it is tested
on the Prairies.

← PRAIRIES ↗

CBC

A company whose government mandate was
to reach as many Canadians as possible.
It has fulfilled its mandate.
More than twenty million Canadians
listen and view its programs daily.
All are employed by the CBC.

I'M AFRAID
WE'RE ALL FULL—
A CBC CAMERA
CREW JUST
CHECKED IN

Convention

  Like it or not, you've got to attend.
It's where you're going to let the party know
that you're the leader with the most.
The most balloons,
the most girls in short skirts,
the most free drinks,
the most delegates
in stupid hats
with your name on them,
the most signs,
and the most
government jobs
to give away.
You'll need to smile
for several days.
This is impossible,
you say?
Not if you use the following:

Fishing Line

  Place line
in mouth (A)

Take ends of
line around and
over ears (B)

Pull line
tight. Tie
in a knot. (C)

Brush hair,
if you have any, over the
line. You're ready for
action.

Just one thing.
You won't be able to eat
for the days the line is in place.
So what?
You probably need to drop
a few pounds, anyway.
All politicians do.

Civil Servant

Despite what you've heard
about them (most of it true)
these are the characters
who know what's going on.
More importantly,
they knew it long before
some young shiny-faced
posh lawyer beat his way
into the big office.

They're everywhere.
Every minister you appoint
will have them.
Remember,
the jobs you give your mates will be
for a limited time only.
For the civil servant,
it's forever.

Long after you and your lot have
taken to your rocking chairs,
these civil servants will be
arranging the papers
on what was your desk
as they see fit.

All the suggestions they make
may turn out to be disastrous,
but they can't be traced back to them.

They don't
have to answer to the government.
They are the government.
The newspapers may carry your picture,
but it will be the undersecretary
who celebrates his twentieth year
in office behind a desk
as big as yours.

· "But I thought we were cutting down on these people?"
you say. We are. With their help.

A civil servant is dealing
with the problem of overstaffing.
He has three assistants,
fourteen secretaries, and
another office.

MINISTER

DEPUTY
MINISTER

Cabinet

A group chosen by you to head up the most important ministeries.

No sense spending your time in office arguing. So choose the ones that are a little slow upstairs.

Bright ones will start to think for themselves and interfere with the civil servants. It'll just give you a headache.

When asked to justify their actions
to an opposition just as ignorant
as they are about running a country,
tell them to say,
"It's true that the government
has moved slowly forward,
but they have moved
as quickly as they know how.
For them to move more rapidly forward
without further knowledge
would mean moving back
at a faster rate
than going forward."

To which there is only one possible answer. "Hear, hear!"

Conservative (as in Progressive)

One of three teams involved.
They are led by a raspy voice
and a long chin.
The team is extremely confident,
since most of them are businessmen
who no longer have time for business.
They have decided to go into politics
and do nothing all day.

Conversation

It's made at parties given for you.
Keep it to a minimum.
Don't forget why you're there;
in order that the greatest number
of people can see you.
So she's got a great figure
and finds you fascinating.
Do you want to be Prime Minister
or don't you?

Don't ask questions. They prompt answers.

Wrong	Right
So what brings you here?	Hi!
Haven't I seen you before somewhere?	Well, hi!
It's nice to see you again. What's doing?	Well, hi there!

SO HE LIED
ABOUT HIS
AGE — I
LIKE THAT
IN A —
PERSON

D

Delegates

People you need
more than your mother or wife.
They decide whether you're
going to get to the big office.
They're everywhere,
which makes it tricky.

DELEGATE

They will all
tell you they are for you.
Don't believe it.
At the convention,
you won't recognize any of them.
Smile at everyone and
squeeze as many elbows as you can.

ELBOW

Tell them all that you've met
and that you remember their promise to you.

If you smile enough they'll believe you.

Most of them are there for the fun
and haven't the faintest idea
who they are going to vote for.
Spontaneous demonstrations
and banners with your name on
should work wonders.

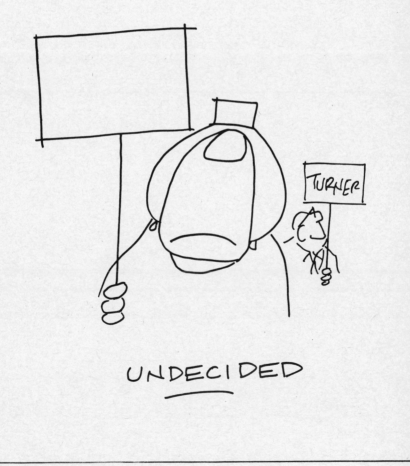

UNDECIDED

Most delegates
will be looking for Knowlton Nash and Lloyd Robertson.
Get close enough to make it look like you
and Lloyd and Knowlton
are old buddies and that if either of them had a vote,
you'd be it.

To win delegates you need:
The best-planned spontaneous demonstration. Free drinks.
The prettiest girls in a spontaneous demonstration. Free drinks.
The loudest band in a spontaneous demonstration. Free drinks.
Good signs, banners, lapel buttons, hats, scarves, and vests.
Free drinks.

What about the issues? What issues?

Debates

They're boooor-ing. A bunch of idiots
(who would love to get the job that you're after)
sitting around telling people
that they know all the answers.

Unfortunately you must show up.
To refuse is to suggest that
you're hiding from something.
So sit and smile.
Look as though you're enjoying it.

And for Pete's sake don't worry
if you say something wrong.
If it's a TV debate,
most people are tuned to something else.
And if it's not, the ones filling
the chairs in the hall are no doubt
just sheltering from the rain.

AN ARMY
OF PACMEN JUST
ATE THE MODERATOR

Democratic

It's the way voting must be seen to be done.
What it means is that each party claws to get to as many
people as they can on voting day.

Elderly people are fought over by the parties.
They are driven to the polling stations
in hired buses.

During the ride
cookies will be passed around
and singsongs take place,
extolling the virtues of the party that
hired the bus.
Passengers are made to feel guilty
should they even think of
another party during the ride.

There's only one hitch:
No one gets a ride back.

WHERE'S
THE
BUS ?

Why should they? They've already voted.

Discrimination

You're against it. Especially if you're a woman.
If you're a man? You're still against it.

There are more than twelve million women out there.
Most of them have the vote.

Suggest changes. Here are a few chestnuts that have proved successful over the years:

Equal pay for work of equal value.

Day care.   Women priests.

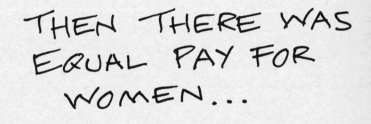

E

Election Day

By the time the day arrives the voter really doesn't care who wins as long as he can get on with his own life.

Western Canadians have a unique advantage
over the rest of the country.
Knowlton Nash will give them the name of the
winner before they set out for the polling station.

Many a voter in Victoria has found himself
in the voting booth while their choice is on TV
in an empty room reserved for a victory party
that didn't happen.

EXCUSE
ME LEAVING—
I HAVE TO GO
AND VOTE

Employment

See "Unemployment"

Economy

Promise that you'll turn it around.

Exclusive

An interview given to the journalist with most clout who favours your ideas.

There's just you and him. Talk about his favourite sport and hand him next week's press release as he leaves.

Editorials

Columns of words read by the publisher of the newspaper in which they appear.

All will begin with a vicious attack on you.

Not to worry. Near the end, a paragraph will begin with the word, "However."

F

Fellow

As in "My fellow Canadians!"
It's an absolute must as an opening remark
(when in Canada).
It implies that the politician
speaking is family:

The father he never had.
The mother they always wanted.
The brother or sister
she dreamed about.

So he won't send
a card at Christmas.
Neither does the rest
of the family.

Fallible

A trait found in all Members of Parliament.
Unable to reach a position of importance
in the outside world, they have turned to politics.
Here they can find kindred spirits.
In their Ottawa offices they can hide
the many problems that stopped them
getting into the boardrooms of the nation.

Outside their offices they can quickly command the rhetoric that hides these flaws from public scrutiny.

The advantage of having the faults that have held them back in private life is that they can quickly recognize them in the members of the opposition, and effectively cajole and deride those across the floor of the House for having those same problems.

PIMPLE FACE

Fuddle-Duddle

It's the kind of swearing that is allowed in the House (not your house, The House).
This particular word is reserved for Prime Ministers.

Here are some others:

Wording Used	Meanings
You, sir, are a cad.	★*!@!
You, sir, are completely without principles.	@*!★!

Farmers

People who live in the country and starve to death feeding the nation.

G

Guzzle

Since they are on a never-ending round
of cocktail parties, most politicians
can develop a drinking problem.
However, it usually goes unnoticed,
since the way they behave after
one drink too many
is similar to the way they behave before
one drink too many.

Governor General

She is a stand-in for the Queen.
She needn't look like the Queen.
Just act like the Queen.

HAND
WAVING
(QUEEN)

HAND
WAVING
(GOVERNOR
GENERAL)

H

House of Commons

It's the very heart of the country.

Where Canadians of every
race, creed, and religion,
rich or poor, can come to see
democracy in action.

Eight hours' drive from Toronto,
twelve hours' drive and an
hour ferry ride from Newfoundland,
and a fourteen-day nonstop drive from Victoria.

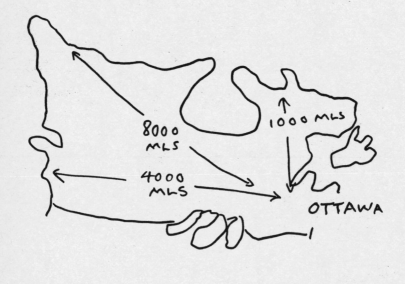

Handshake (General)

Use both hands. This way you are in control and can pry yourself loose when you have to.

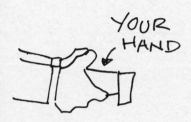 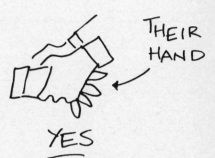

Handshake (Strangers of Voting Age)

From out of right field swing one hand in the general direction of their outstretched hand. Make as little contact as possible.

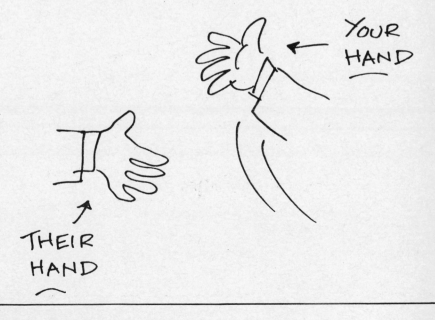

Honours List

It's the Queen's shopping list.
Instead of writing '5 kg. of potatoes,'
the Queen will write down
a name and place letters after it.

Some years ago,
Canadians decided to write up
a list of their own.

The Prime Minister
immediately called the Queen.
"No problem, my dear.
And while you're about it,
pick me up a half a dozen eggs.

MR SMITH, MR JONES —
HE DOESN'T HAVE THE
ORDER OF CANADA
EITHER

I

Inflation

Tell people that you are going to
make it go down.
It will go up.
The only way to make it go down
is to stop spending money.
Thatcher and Reagan decided
that they would spend less
on those who had the least clout.

Since most Canadians have little clout
it is difficult to decide who to miss
when the money is given out.
Be democratic.
Miss 'em all.

Influence

Something that allows someone to get close
to the kind of people that you can't.

Since the someone who has it is one
of the people you can't get to,
you'll need an introduction –
by someone else who has it.

HOW COME THIS
REFERENCE FROM THE
QUEEN IS IN THE SAME
HAND-WRITING AS THE
ONE FROM THE POPE?

Immigrant

Someone who feels that coming here
is better than staying there.
They have impossible names to spell.
Their descendants end up as senators
from western Canada or
morning talk-show hosts.

They get "landed immigrant"
stamped in their passports.
This proves to the customs officers
that they are immigrants
and have landed.

Since they are not allowed to vote
you can ignore their many problems.
However,
many become Canadian citizens,
so a smile or two in their direction
can pay dividends at a later date.

Interpreter

If Eugene Whelan didn't need one, neither do you.

Idiots

Those who suggest that what you
recommend is not good for Canada.
All are in the opposition parties.
Suffer them kindly.
They have been known to
come to their senses and cross
the floor to join your party.
Do you need an idiot in your ranks?
Don't be silly.
Once they've crossed the floor
they'll no longer be idiots,
idiot.

... SO, SICK OF
THE JUNGLE, YOU
DECIDE TO LEAVE
TARZAN AND GO
INTO POLITICS

Interest Rates

Something that goes up.

Interview

For a politician to get elected,
he must be seen by his public.

There is only one way of doing this.
Submit to a cross-examination
in front of millions of people.
The television interviewer can be brutal,
taunting, and insolent.
The candidate must be
serious yet friendly.

Question

A piercing one that has caught the politician completely off guard.

DO YOU HAVE A MISTRESS?

Answer

Throw back the head, and give a good chuckle. This gains valuable time for you to think of an answer. If the chuckle is long enough the viewer will not only lose interest in the answer, but forget the question.

Split the question into parts. ("Yes, of course, but there are two ways of looking at that . . ."). Now the interviewer is stumped, since he had no idea that there was one satisfactory answer, let alone two.

HA HA HO HE HA

Then there is the attacking answer: "When have you ever been responsible for the jobs of five million people with a budget of $58 million?" (Be careful to smile after a remark like this. You're attacking the interviewer, not the viewers.) Don't let an interviewer get away with innuendo:

Q: "I've heard it said, Prime Minister, that . . ."
A: "Who said? Come on, out with it . . . name names!"

And remember, the greatest enemy of television is time. When searching for an answer, start with: "Actually, there are nine points to your question. Point one . . ." "Back to the studio" should come by the end of point two, if not sooner.

J

Justify

It's a fancy word for
"What the hell do you mean by that?"
You're the Prime Minister and there
is no reason why you
should explain to anyone
why you did what you did.

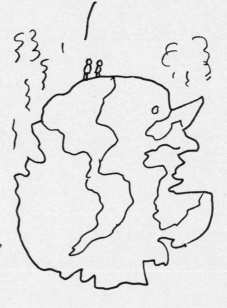

I WAS ACTING
UNDER ORDERS

But if you want to try,
be careful.
If something you've done
has proven a complete mess,
"I was acting under orders"
is not a good answer.

On the other hand,
"Someone failed to carry out my orders"
is the perfect justification.

K

Kissing

It's for kissing babies and wives.
Other people's babies,
not someone else's wife.
It's done as a gesture of
love of all mankind.
The act immediately signals that
the politician doing the kissing
can't be all bad,
despite what the voter may
have heard to the contrary.

Not every baby in sight has to be kissed.
Naturally a baby with visible signs of
contagious disease can be avoided.

Be sure that the mother holding the baby
is the rightful mother.
It's quite common for complete strangers
to grab babies and hold them to
be kissed in order to get their pictures
in the local newspaper.

The real mother could quite rightly
hold the politician responsible
for the "temporary" kidnapping of her baby.
This kind of publicity
is not good for a politician.

REAL
MOTHER
AND CHILD

FAKE
MOTHER
AND CHILD

L

Leader

Must enjoy travel and the good life.
Must be able to speak two languages.
Preferably English and French.
Can wear expensive clothes
in such a way that they appear inexpensive
to the average unemployed voter.
Must smile at any leader of a country
more important than Canada.

BAD

GOOD

Lose

Something that's about to
happen to your opponent.
Find the scruffiest people
in each town you visit.
Give each one an empty wine bottle.
Now pin a button on their lapel.
Your opponent's button.

Lose (as in Deposit)

Too many people finding out the truth about you and deciding to vote for someone else.

Leaks

Ugly stories about your opponents given to the press. The uglier, the better. If you haven't got any stories, make them up.

HE DRESSES LIKE BOY GEORGE

M

Ministers

You give out these plum appointments, so if you want someone to do something for you just drop a hint.

"Fred in Finance has been under the weather lately."

"Oh dear. Sorry to hear that, Prime Minister. Can I freshen your drink?"

"No thanks. But I wouldn't mind the old lawn getting the once-over with the mower . . ."

You get the idea.

I'M CONCERNED THAT MY UPWARD MOBILITY HAS BOTTOMED OUT

Morals

All politicians have them until they're found out.

Machine (as in Party Machine)

A crowd from the same side that shouts about the virtues
of the group they belong to.

The machine in power has an advantage,
since they can use the taxpayers' money
to shout through the media
about how great they are.
Since these are paid ads, most newspapers
tend to ignore them.
Unless the publisher is
part of another party machine.

Mountie

Someone who will salute you
the moment you get within spitting distance.
You don't need to return the salute
unless you're wearing a hat.

If you don't know how to salute, take your hat off
before you get to him.

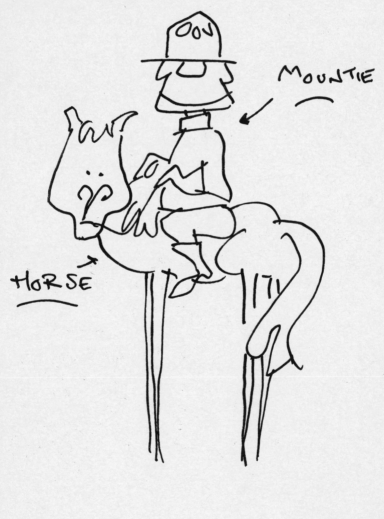

HI
THERE
FRANK,
OR IS
IT
CHARLES ?

MP

Short for Member of Parliament.
Constantly criticized and held up
to ridicule by the press and,
in particular,
by cartoonists.
It's difficult to know why a person
would ever want the job.

WHAT ARE YOU—
SOME KIND
OF NUT ?

On closer look, however,
it's not so surprising.
The pay is good.
And although they constantly ask
everyone to knuckle down
and get on with it,
they do not begin work
until after lunch,
never work weekends,
and take three long holidays a year.

Phones, letters, and travel
are thrown in free,
and the parliamentary
cafeteria dishes up
food fit for a king at
McDonald's prices.

But most of all it gives an MP the appearance
of importance without having to achieve it.

EARTH TO PLUTO—
NO SIGN OF INTELLIGENT
LIFE—OVER

Majority

You want it.

Minority

Could be better.

Monarch

Better known as the Queen.
She's the one person everyone loves.
The one person trusted by the
general and the private.
The bishop and the clergy.
The Chairman of the Board
and the clerk.

The one person that can make sure
that every decision made
in the House of Commons
is in the best interests of the people.

A QUEEN

Unfortunately, she is 6,000 miles away and has
enough problems with her own House of Commons.

N

News Conference

Any place where two or more journalists
are gathered together
(not counting the Press Club).
The idea is to tell all the press
what you are planning to do
instead of having to repeat yourself
for every reporter.

FOR STARTERS, YOU
CAN STOP BELIEVING
EVERYTHING YOU
READ IN THE NEWS-
PAPERS

If a reporter
comes up with a tricky question,
you can pass it off
with a little buttering up.
Using the reporter's name is good.
Especially his or her first name.

"Well Charles. I'm pleased you asked that."
(You're not, but it will
immediately disarm Charles,
who is still pleased as punch
that his Mum and Dad in Kamloops
have seen their son addressed by
the Prime Minister as "Charles.")

Any answer will do.
The last thing he wants to lose is this
new-found friendship with a VIP.

WELL, IF IT
ISN'T CHARLES—
HOW'S YOUR
MUM?

Names

As Prime Minister you're going to find
lots of overnight close friends.
All potential fund-raising dinner pals.
You can't remember names?
Of course you can.

Their Name	Your Name for Them
Robertson Evans	Hi there, fellow.
A big Robertson Evans	Hi there, big fellow.
Sybil Stocks	My dear
A big Sybil Stocks	My dear

NATO

The North Atlantic Treaty Organization.
A group of countries who got together to
decide where the next war would be held.
The biggest of these countries decided to
hold it in Europe.

The biggest of these countries is not in Europe.

NDP

The party that everyone says they will
vote for but nobody ever does.
They're on the side of the working man,
which are most people in the country.

So why don't they vote NDP? What, and waste their vote?

O

Official Portrait

It's a painting of you. It will hang in a gallery in the House of Commons.

You will not like it.

IT MAY BE UGLY, BUT IT'S A VERY GOOD LIKENESS

Opinion Polls

Something to be ignored, unless they're in your favour.

Opposition

They sit opposite you in the House of Commons.
Whatever you say they're going to be against it,
so don't waste your time with them.
If they don't like what you're proposing,
too bad. You're going to get it passed anyway.

You have more people on your side
than they do on theirs.
How else did you get to be Prime Minister?

Optimism

It's how you view the future.
Everything is going to be great
"in the near future."
Or, if things look really bad,
"Everything is going to be great
in the not too distant future."

Outcome

A disappointment.
Since you will be instituting
the legislation for change,
the finger can point at you when
the outcome is not what
you had planned.
Never mind.
Put out more of the same.
The more the better.
So one's a disappointment.
There's plenty more legislation
where that came from.

Optimist

Anyone who feels that buying this book will help them
get the job of Prime Minister.

P

Party

There are three.
You'll have to decide
which one you want to join
before you can become Prime Minister.
There has never been a Prime Minister
who did not belong to one or the other.

You *can* run as an Independent.
This means that the only party
you favour is your own party of one.
The advantage is that if
your party does win an election,
you can pick yourself unanimously
to be Prime Minister.

THE POPE
ISN'T
RUNNING

Press

At one time they could be seen in the Press Gallery.
No longer. Now the television cameras
can carry the House to them.
In their offices where they are
too busy to watch,
or in the Press Club
where they are too busy
bending their elbows.

So how do they know what's going on?
Through you. Just give them
what you want them to know.

One word of warning.
Watch out for court reporters
and rock critics.
You too could be "Watergated."

Public Relations

The true role of the politician.
While the civil servants run the country,
the politician attempts to distract the public.

You can do this in a variety of ways.
You can spend tax money on
ads in the newspapers.
You can take government planes
across the country to
get the message through.

In each of these stops, take to television
for that little extra push.
How will you have the time?
Because, as I said in the beginning,
the civil servants run the country.

THINGS GO
BETTER WITH
US

Party

The clinking glasses kind.

You'll need to be selective.
No friends.
You can see them any time.
And don't go by size.
Better a party of ten possible supporters,
than a rally of 1,000 underage Boy Scouts.

Phone

You'll need eighty-five.
One for each secretary,
and one in the car.
This is in case of a nuclear attack.
As Prime Minister you'll need
to know that one is on its way.
Make sure all world leaders
have the number.
It could be awkward.

"Information?
I'm trying to get the phone number
of your Prime Minister."
The familiar voice of the ex-movie star
came down the line.

"Do you have an address?"

"It's at the intersection of Sparks Street
and Wellington, Ottawa."

"We have a Thunderbird listed under 'Mike Duffy' just leaving the National Press Club."

"No. This is a bulletproof car."

"Are you sure of the intersection?"

"The lights could have changed by now. Can you try Sussex Drive and Wellington?"

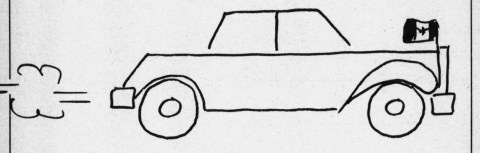

"Ah! Here it is. Would you like me to connect you?"

"Yes please, and hurry."

"Prime Minister's car here."

"This is the President. Let me speak to the Prime Minister, please."

"Hold the line please."

"Prime Minister's secretary here."

"I'd like to speak to the Prime Minister, please."

"I'll put you through."

"Prime Minister's personal secretary speaking."

"I want to speak to the Prime Minister."

"Prime Minister's private secretary here."

"Get me the damn Prime Minister."

"I'm sorry, sir. He's in a meeting."

Peace

You're for it. You're not for them.
They parade up and down the street
telling you what you should do about peace.
You're in charge and no one tells you what to do.

If you want to talk about peace
and test a neutron bomb over Moose Jaw,
that's what you're going to do.
Just don't do it at rush hour.

DON'T BE SILLY—
AS LONG AS BOTH
SIDES ARE STRONG
AND POWERFUL,
THERE'S NO WAY
WE'LL BECOME
EXTINCT

Political Cartoonist

A person who draws ugly pictures of you
and says nasty things about you.
You have to laugh and ask for the original
to put up on your office wall.

Poverty

You don't like it. Promise to wipe it out . . .
along with war, pollution, unemployment, and prostitution.

HOW MUCH
WILL IT COST
IF I DON'T
WIPE YOU
OUT?

Q

Question Period

You'll be giving answers.
So why isn't it called the Answer Period? I don't know.

You'll need to keep awake.
Some people will be making snide
remarks about the job you're doing.
They're all after your job and are
a little ticked off that they haven't got it.

If you don't know the answer get someone else
to stand up and field the question.

Just one thing:
Make sure the one you finger for the job
is a member of your party.

R

Religion

It's an absolute must.
Any politician separating himself
from the great upstairs is doomed to fail.
Whether the voter believes
or not is immaterial.
The politicians he picks have got
to have God firmly on their side.

When the man that he has voted for
arrives in Ottawa, City of Sin,
he's going to need all the help he can get.

Rostrum

It's a platform that allows you to speak
and be seen while you are doing it.

Don't approach it with caution.
When called upon to speak,
run, don't walk.
Take the steps leading to the rostrum
at least two at a time.

The people want to know you're fit enough for
the job of Prime Minister.

S

Senate

It has two functions.
One is to give an opinion on certain bills
being suggested by the House.
The other is to say yes or yes as to
whether the bill should be allowed to pass.

IT WAS TERRIBLE—
I DREAMT I WAS
GIVING A SPEECH IN
THE SENATE AND WOKE
UP AND FOUND I WAS

Sex

A politician's most dreaded word.
Especially outside of marriage.
Those not married are also expected
to keep away from it.

For voters to see you getting involved in
something that they are denied
is viewed as extremely unfair.
Especially as it was the voters
who gave you the power that attracts
the opposite sex.

Show Business

What has that got to do
with you becoming Prime Minister?
Plenty. Get a well-known face on your side
and you'll be off to the races.

The star will draw the crowd.
Then, before they know what hit them,
you can stand up and deliver a speech.

Sexist

To be against
one sex by favouring
the other sex,
provided that the
other sex is your sex
and not the other sex.

Supreme Court

You may think that once you're the Prime Minister
you'll be able to lord it over all you survey.
It should be like that. But it isn't.
The Supreme Court do their own thing
whether you like it or not.

GUILTY OR NOT
GUILTY, PRIME
MINISTER?

A bunch of judges,
one a woman,
sit down to listen to people argue
that the learned judges
they've already seen
ain't so learned after all.

So why do people take their case
to the Supreme Court?
Lawyers have to make a living
somehow.

Speaking

You're not being paid to do it,
but pretend you're happy to be
wherever it is you're doing it.
Give the impression that they'll
all be invited over to the house
once you're in Sussex Drive.
Find out what they want
and tell them that's what you're
going to give them.

Whatever the first language of the group
you're speaking to is, say goodbye in it.
If they're from a Greek community,
give them a Greek farewell.
I don't know what it is. Find out.

Separation

Parts of Canada think they can get a
better deal going it on their own.
If you let them try it you will have
a smaller country to be a head of.
This can result in a decrease in your salary.
Tell them that they have to stay and
suffer like the rest of us.

Student

Someone whom you promise to get a job.

Speaker

One who doesn't speak.
He sits in the House among the screaming mobs
and tries to keep order.
Sometimes he succeeds.

His chair is known as the Speaker's chair.
It's a high-backed wooden chair made
deliberately uncomfortable to stop
the Speaker from going to sleep.

The Speaker is required to know
the name of everyone in the House . . .
and where they come from.
To wave a hand in the general
direction of someone and say
"What's-his-name from thingumabob"
will hardly do.

YOU — THE ONE
JUMPING UP
AND DOWN ON
HIS DESK

So the Speaker sits up nights
going over the names one by one.
As soon as he has memorized a new name,
that MP is pointed to
and told to get up and speak.
Even if he doesn't want to speak.

To refuse to speak when the Speaker
tells you to is the height of bad manners.
It is also an insult to the Speaker.
Since he has been
chosen for his good memory,
any chance of you speaking again
has gone out the window . . .
along with the chance of re-election.

T

Truth

Something that doesn't concern you.

Tourists

They arrive in the spring.
Many will want to take your picture.
Still more will want you to take pictures of them.

Trade and Commerce

They sell whatever we feel the rest
of the world needs and can't get.
Like Candu reactors and other household items.

U

Undecided

Most people interviewed by pollsters.

"And who will you be voting for, sir?"

"I haven't decided."

"Are you a delegate?"

"I think so."

"Are you going to the convention?"

"It's quite possible."

"So you'll decide when you get there?"

"Get where?"

Underdog

Everyone but you.

Unemployment

"See "Employment"

THE JOBS BEEN FILLED BUT IF YOU DON'T MIND WAITING...

Underpaid

They're the ones who carry placards and
walk up and down outside your window.
It's an ugly sight.
If you feel you
have to do something,
pull the drapes.

Understate

Figures, mainly.
Unemployment figures . . .
spending figures . . .
inflation . . .
the opposition's latest poll
in the popularity stakes . . .

V

Victory

What everyone wants but only you have.
Unfortunately not everyone will
be aware that you have it,
as your opponent will
be smiling and giving speeches,
just as you are.

His supporters will be shouting,
jumping, and screaming,
just as yours are.

It's important that you let everyone
know that you are It,
and not the ninny down the street,
who's talking about next time.

There will be a next time.
But not for him.

MACKENZIE
KING
AIN'T
RUNNING

Voters

The people who decide
whether or not you should get
$135,000 a year expenses paid.

If you happen to live in a
part of the country that can't
stand the party you head,
you've had the biscuit.

By the same token,
any idiot can make it to the top
if he finds himself heading
a party that is popular in his area.

That's why leaders
pick their areas very carefully.
"Who had the three million
majority last time out?
That's the area for me . . .
where did you say it was again?"

THIS FELLOW YOU'RE PUSHING — IS HE WHITE OR GREEN?

W

Whistle Stop

Any place that you visit that you've never heard of, and will never visit again once you're elected.

Women

As a man,
you like them.
In fact, some of your best
friends are women.

All women
have had a raw deal
and you're going to do everything
you can to make it easier
for women to advance
(short of into your job).

Many feel that
once women get equality
it will destroy their
charm and beauty.
Women will take on a
tougher stance and
adopt the lean and hungry
look of ambition.
This is true.

The women sharing the
House of Commons with you
are good examples.
One of their tirades aimed
in your direction can be
extremely damaging,
unless you turn it aside with tact.

Wait for her to finish.
Before she can sit down,
rush across the House and
pull out her chair for her.

CONGRATULATIONS—
IT'S A FEMINIST

WAVE

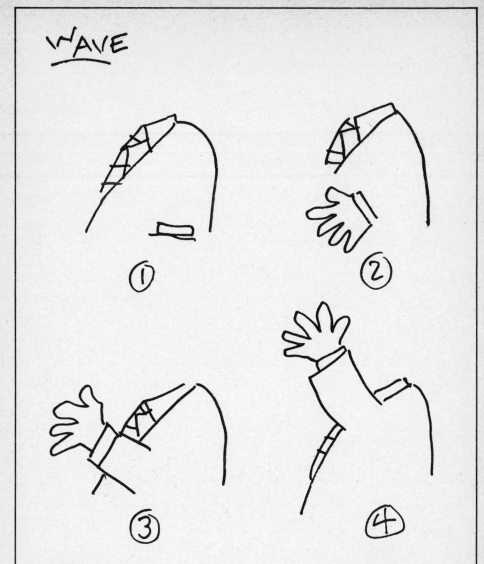

Wave

The wave is seen as a friendly gesture.
It is absolutely essential to a Prime Minister.
It gives the impression you have
a great number of friends.

Anyone with so many friends can't be all bad.

Wife

She's the one standing beside you.

She is required to smile
like a Cheshire cat with a face-lift.
She must be seen and not heard
during your term of office.

She must give the impression that you two
are as happy today as on your wedding day.

This is not hard to accomplish,
as she has been packed away like her
wedding dress since you entered politics.

War

A no-no.

You don't care
who has invaded wherever.
You are deeply disturbed
at the news.
That's it.

X

X

Marks the spot.
The names of those running in an
election are spelled out.
All it requires is an X beside
the one the voter likes.

Voters like the name they have
seen on most people's lawns.

Those elected to office are the
ones with the most friends
who own a front lawn.

ME
for
P.M.

I WAS
WONDERING
IF YOU COULD
DO ME A
FAVOUR ?

Y

Yukon

The fellow who takes care of their affairs
looks like Leslie Neilson, the actor.
What has this got to do
with being Prime Minister?
Nothing,
but I'm trying to fill out the Ys.

Z

Zenith

    It's the pinnacle.
The top.
It's the pot of gold
at the end of the rainbow.
No more bowing.
No more scraping.

    Voters can phone,
write letters,
attempt to see you.
You haven't got the time.

    One word of warning:
Zenith is one step away from Zero.
Which is one step away from
absolute Zero.
Which is one step
away from Apathy.

NEXT!

A

Apathy

It's a disease . . .